Who Is God?

Loveland, Colorado

Group's R.E.A.L. Guarantee to you:

This Group resource incorporates our R.E.A.L. approach to ministry—one that encourages long-term retention and life transformation. It's ministry that's:

Relational
Because learner-to-learner interaction enhances learning and builds Christian friendships.

Experiential
Because what learners experience through discussion and action sticks with them up to 9 times longer than what they simply hear or read.

Applicable
Because the aim of Christian education is to equip learners to be both hearers and doers of God's Word.

Learner-based
Because learners understand and retain more when the learning process takes into consideration how they learn best.

Who Is God?

Junior High Bible Study Series

Visit our Web site: **www.grouppublishing.com**

Credits
Contributing Authors: Tammy L. Bicket, Bob Buller, Darrell Pearson, and Amy Simpson
Editors: Tammy L. Bicket and Dawn M. Brandon
Creative Development Editor: Amy Simpson
Chief Creative Officer: Joani Schultz
Copy Editor: Betty Taylor
Art Director: Sharon Anderson
Print Production Artist: Joyce Douglas
Cover Art Director/Designer: Jeff A. Storm
Cover Photographer: Daniel Treat
Production Manager: DeAnne Lear

ISBN 0-7644-2498-X
10 9 8 7 6 5 4 3 2 1 12 11 10 09 08 07 06 05 04 03

Printed in the United States of America.

Table of Contents

Who Is God?

God is not some stern, distant, unknowable judge waiting to punish teenagers when they don't measure up. He is a loving God who wants to help them and to be intimately involved in their daily lives.

Who is God? That's a question philosophers and theologians have pondered for centuries. Many people seek the answer to this question. Many religions believe conflicting answers.

Junior high students may know much about what God does. Now it's time for them to really know who he is. God is not some stern, distant, unknowable judge waiting to punish teenagers when they don't measure up. He is a loving God who wants to help them and to be intimately involved in their daily lives.

In this book, teenagers will come face to face with the God who loves them. In the first study, they'll learn that even in the chaos of an uncertain world, God the Father is in control and knows what he's doing. Best of all, he's working for their good even through difficulties.

In the second study, students will learn that God the Son, Jesus, is their best friend.

In the third study, teenagers will discover the many ways in which God the Holy Spirit helps and encourages them.

Finally, they'll see that God is the one who defines what is right. They'll also learn how each member of the Trinity helps us recognize and implement those standards of righteousness.

Who God is doesn't have to be a mystery. God truly wants us to know him on a personal basis. He has left his signature and signs of who he is all around us—in nature, in everything he has created, in his Word, and in whispered words of love to our hearts. Now your teenagers can know him intimately and truly return his love.

junior high bible study series

About Faith 4 Life

Use Faith 4 Life studies to show your teenagers how the Bible is relevant to their lives. Help them see that God can invade every area of their lives and change them in ways they can only imagine. Encourage your students to go deeper into faith—faith that will sustain them for life! Faith 4 Life, forever!

Faith 4 Life: Junior High Bible Study Series helps young teenagers take a Bible-based approach to faith and life issues. Each book in the series contains these important elements:

- **Life application of Bible truth**—Faith 4 Life studies help teenagers understand what the Bible says and then apply that truth to their lives.
- **A relevant topic**—Each Faith 4 Life book focuses on one main topic, with four studies to give your students a thorough understanding of how the Bible relates to that topic. These topics were chosen by youth leaders as the ones most relevant for junior high-age students.
- **One point**—Each study makes one point, centering on that one theme to make sure students really understand the important truth it conveys. This point is stated upfront and throughout the study.
- **Simplicity**—The studies are easy to use. Each contains a "Before the Study" box that outlines any advance preparation required. Each study also contains a "Study at a Glance" chart so that you can quickly and easily see what supplies you'll need and what each study will involve.
- **Action and interaction**—Each study relies on experiential learning to help students learn what God's Word has to say. Teenagers discuss and debrief their experiences in large groups, small groups, and individual reflection.
- **Reproducible handouts**—Faith 4 Life books include reproducible handouts for students. No need for student books!
- **Tips, tips, and more tips**—Faith 4 Life studies are full of "FYI" tips for the teacher, providing extra ideas, insights into young people, and hints for making the studies go smoothly.
- **Flexibility**—Faith 4 Life studies include optional activities and bonus activities. Use a study as it's written, or use these options to create the study that works best for your group.
- **Follow-up ideas**—At the end of each book, you'll find a section called "Changed 4 Life." This section provides ideas for following up with your students to make sure the Bible truths stick with them.

God: Master of Life's Puzzle

Today's teenagers live in a chaotic and uncertain world: divorced and blended families, violence on the streets and in the schools, poverty, abusive parents, pressure to conform, media images assaulting them from every side, and the threat of terrorism and war. Fortunately, the chaos is more apparent than real. God stands in the midst of this world's insanity, calmly and consistently accomplishing his will. Because God sees everything, nothing catches him by surprise. Because God is firmly in control, nothing can frustrate his plans. And because God always knows what's best, we can trust him to lead us even in chaotic times.

This study encourages teenagers to trust God during chaotic times by helping them see how God can transform even the worst of situations into something good.

The Point

▶ God is in control and knows what he's doing.

Scripture Source

Proverbs 3:5-6

God directs the lives of people who trust in him.

Acts 6:8-15; 7:51-8:8

God uses Stephen's death to spread the gospel.

James 1:2-5

James encourages us to ask God for wisdom so we can learn from life's trials.

The Study at a Glance

Warm-Up (5-10 minutes)

Puzzle Mania

What students will do: Try to put together a puzzle while wearing blindfolds.

Needs: ❑ "Person-Shaped Puzzle" handouts (p. 18)
❑ blindfolds

Optional Activity (5-10 minutes)

What students will do: Try to put together a jigsaw puzzle with pieces face down and without being able to see the picture on the box.

Needs: ❑ 100-piece puzzles

Bible Connection (20-25 minutes)

Stephen's Story

What students will do: Tell the story of Stephen's life in coded messages and discover how God completed the puzzle of Stephen's life through his death.

Needs: ❑ Bibles ❑ newsprint
❑ markers ❑ tape
❑ paper ❑ pencils

Life Application

My Chaos, God's Wisdom (15-20 minutes)

What students will do: Learn how God can turn their chaotic situations into good things.

Needs: ❑ Bibles ❑ markers
❑ index cards

I'm Praying for You (up to 5 minutes)

What students will do: Ask God to help others deal with the chaos in their lives.

Needs: ❑ Bibles ❑ markers

Bonus Activity (10-15 minutes)

What students will do: Examine Isaiah 46:9-11 and discuss how they can be sure God is still in control and knows what he's doing, even when the world around us seems out of control.

Before the Study

Photocopy and cut apart the "Person-Shaped Puzzle" (p. 18) for the "Puzzle Mania" activity. You'll need one copy for every seven students.

List various chaotic situations that junior high teenagers may face. Write each situation on a separate sheet of paper, and hang the papers around the room. For example, you might write situations such as the following:

- Your parents divorce.
- You have problems at school.
- You break up with your boyfriend or girlfriend.
- You go to a new school.
- Your parent loses a job.
- A friend dies.
- You move to a new community.
- A family member joins the military and is sent to a war zone.
- You get into trouble with the police.
- You lose a friend.
- You run away from home.

Warm-Up

Puzzle Mania

(5 to 10 minutes)

Blindfold everyone, and give each person a piece of the puzzle from the "Person-Shaped Puzzle" handout (p. 18). Tell teenagers they have three minutes to assemble the puzzle on the floor. Teenagers can talk to one another and try to put the pieces together by feeling the edges, but they cannot remove their blindfolds.

After three minutes, instruct teenagers to stop and remove their blindfolds.

Form groups of four, and instruct group members to discuss these questions:

- **What was it like trying to put together a puzzle without seeing?**
- **How long do you think it would take you to put together the puzzle in this way?**
- **How is putting together this puzzle like putting together the "pieces" of your life?**
- **In what ways is your life like a puzzle? In what ways is it different?**

FYI If students successfully assembled the puzzle in three minutes, omit the second discussion question.

■ What things make it hard for you to put together the pieces of your life?

After a few minutes of group discussion, bring all teenagers back together and

SAY:

■ Sometimes our lives are so full of chaos and uncertainty that we feel out of control. We don't know how all the pieces of our lives fit together or even if we have all the pieces. We'll learn today, however, that no matter how confusing life seems to us, God is in control and knows what he's doing.

◀ **The Point**

FYI

If you had teenagers try to put together an incomplete puzzle, ask:

■ **How is a puzzle with missing pieces like your life? How is it unlike your life?**

Although the puzzle has seven pieces, the activity will work for a group of any size. If you have puzzle pieces left after you give each person one piece, distribute the extra pieces so some teenagers have more than one. You may want to keep one or two of the extra pieces so teenagers are trying to put together an incomplete puzzle. If you have more than seven teenagers in your group, make several copies of the handout, and have teenagers attempt to put together several puzzles at the same time.

* Optional Activity

(5 to 10 minutes)

Instead of doing the "Puzzle Mania" activity, divide the class into small groups and give each group a 100-piece puzzle. Don't let kids see the picture on the puzzle box. Lay out the puzzle pieces upside down so students can't guess the picture or match colors and patterns. They are not to turn the pieces over or to peek at the other side. Let them experience the frustration of working without really knowing what the final picture will be. After several minutes, let students use the picture on the box and turn over the pieces.

ASK:

■ Why is it easier to work on the puzzle now?

■ Do you still believe the puzzle had the potential to make a complete, attractive picture even when you couldn't see the picture or the colors?

SAY:

■ Sometimes the pieces of our lives seem as confusing and purposeless as these upside-down puzzle pieces. But we can trust that even when we can't, God sees the patterns, the colors, and the final picture he has painted for our lives.

Bible Connection

Stephen's Story

(20 to 25 minutes)

SAY:

- **Sometimes when we're in the middle of chaotic situations, it's hard to see that God is in control of our lives. However, we often can see what God has been doing after all the pieces come together. To learn how to put together the puzzle pieces of our lives, let's examine the puzzle of Stephen's life.**

Have teenagers in each foursome number off from one to four and form new groups. Send all the ones to one area of the room, the twos to another area, and so on. Instruct each group to read one of these four passages: Acts 6:8-10; Acts 6:11-15; Acts 7:51-56; and Acts 7:57–8:1.

While the groups are reading, draw a five-piece puzzle on a sheet of newsprint (see diagram in the margin). Write "Acts 6:8-10" on one piece, "Acts 6:11-15" on another, and so on. (Later in the activity, you'll write in the blank area.) Then write the following questions in the appropriate areas of the puzzle, and hang the newsprint where everyone can see it.

•What was Stephen's situation? (Acts 6:11-15)
•Who was Stephen? (Acts 6:8-10)
• What was Stephen's response? (Acts 7:51-56)
• What happened to Stephen? (Acts 7:57–8:1)

- **Who was Stephen?** (Acts 6:8-10)
- **What was Stephen's situation?** (Acts 6:11-15)
- **What was Stephen's response?** (Acts 7:51-56)
- **What happened to Stephen?** (Acts 7:57–8:1)

SAY:

- **Just as there are different kinds of chaotic experiences, there are different kinds of puzzles. A code is one kind of puzzle. Let's use coded messages to solve the puzzle of Stephen's life.**

Instruct each group to compose a one-sentence answer to its assigned question and then translate the answer into a coded message. Assign the following codes to the groups:

- Group 1: A = 2, B = 4, C = 6, and so on
- Group 2: A = 26, B = 25, C = 24, and so on
- Group 3: A = 0, B = 1, C = 2, and so on
- Group 4: A = 25, B = 24, C = 23, and so on

After groups have encoded their answers, have them write the coded messages on the appropriate sections of the newsprint.

Next, give each group a sheet of paper and a pencil, and have teenagers race to decipher other groups' messages without revealing their own codes. After five minutes, have groups reveal messages that haven't been deciphered.

Have teenagers return to their original groups of four and discuss these questions.

ASK:

- **What was difficult about trying to break the code?**
- **How is this like what Stephen might have felt in his situation?**
- **What parts of Stephen's life seem to have been chaotic?**
- **How did Stephen respond to the chaos in his life?**
- **How would you have reacted if you had been in Stephen's situation?**
- **Do you think Stephen knew how the pieces of his life fit together? Explain.**
- **How are you like Stephen? How are you unlike him?**
- **To what extent was Stephen's life out of his control? out of God's control?**
- **Why do you think God allowed angry men to kill Stephen?**
- **Why do you think God lets chaotic things happen in your life?**

SAY:

- **Contrary to what we may expect, the puzzle of Stephen's life wasn't finished when he died. One important piece remained to be put into place. In your group, read Acts 8:1-8 to discover what that piece was.**

While groups are reading, write, "Acts 8:1-8" on the blank puzzle piece on the newsprint.

ASK:

- **What good came of Stephen's death?**

Write teenagers' responses in the appropriate space on the newsprint. Then

SAY:

- **Stephen probably didn't understand why God let him die, but Stephen did know that God is in control and knows what he's doing. God used the chaos of Stephen's life and death to** ◀ **The Point**

FYI

If you want groups to translate their answers into the coded messages more quickly, consider writing out each code on a sheet of paper and giving each group the appropriate code.

FYI

If teenagers have trouble deciphering the codes, offer to help them. For example, you could tell teenagers that M equals 26 in Group 1's message, 14 in Group 2's message, 12 in Group 3's message, and 13 in Group 4's message. After another minute, you could add that S equals 38 in Group 1's message, 8 in Group 2's message, 18 in Group 3's message, and 7 in Group 4's message.

draw others to Christ. He can use the chaotic situations of your life to accomplish something good too.

Life Application

My Chaos, God's Wisdom

(15 to 20 minutes)

Distribute markers of various colors and index cards. Tell teenagers to draw on the cards symbols that somehow represent who they are. For example, one person might draw a happy face because he likes to smile, and another might sketch a tennis shoe because she plays racquet sports.

After teenagers create their symbols, instruct them to walk around the room and read the descriptions of the situations you've hung up in the room before the meeting. As they do so, they should draw their symbols on the papers that describe situations in their lives. Give teenagers at least three minutes to put their symbols on the situation papers.

Have teenagers re-form their original foursomes and discuss these questions in their groups:

- **How does it feel to be surrounded by so many chaotic situations?**
- **What did this activity reveal about your life? about the lives of others in the group?**
- **How is the chaotic appearance of the papers like the chaotic appearance of our lives? How is it different?**
- **Based on all this chaos, how can we know that God is in control and knows what he's doing?** ◀ **The Point**

Instruct groups to read Proverbs 3:5-6 and James 1:2-5. Then have group members discuss the following questions.

ASK:

- **Can you think of a time you went through a chaotic situation that God turned into something good? Explain.**
- **How can God turn our chaotic experiences into good things?**
- **What can God's wisdom do for us when we're going through chaotic times?**

FYI Encourage teenagers to put their symbols on as many situation papers as apply to them, but assure them that they don't need to mark any that they would prefer to keep private. You also may want to provide blank sheets of paper, a marker, and tape so teenagers can add any situations you might have forgotten. Tell teenagers to write any chaotic situation you've missed on a sheet of paper and hang it near the other papers.

SAY:

■ **Everyone has to deal with chaos in his or her life. But Christians can ask God for the wisdom to survive and even thrive in chaos. And whether or not we ever understand why we go through difficult times, we can always be certain that God is in control and knows what he's doing.**

The Point ▶

I'm Praying for You

(up to 5 minutes)

Give everyone a marker.

SAY:

■ **On the back of your index card, write one chaotic situation you're facing currently.**

Give teenagers a moment to do this. Then

SAY:

■ **Now write a question you'd like God to answer about that situation. For example, you may want God to help you understand why you're going through the situation or what you're supposed to do. If you don't mind someone else knowing about your situation, sign your card. If you prefer, you may use your symbol or leave your card unsigned. When you've finished writing, put your card with the others in a pile in the center of the room.**

After everyone has put a card in the pile, mix the cards. Have everyone take a card (not his or her own), find a private area, and pray for the situation and the question written on the card. Encourage teenagers to take home the cards they've selected as reminders to pray for one another through the chaotic situations they all face.

FYI

When James promises that God will give "wisdom" to anyone who asks for it, he probably is referring to wisdom in the midst of troubles (see James 1:2-4). At the very least, God will show us how to respond when we face troubles. God may also help us understand the nature and the purpose of our struggles. However, we may never fully comprehend why God allows us to undergo trials. For example, Job never understood why his world crumbled. Whatever our level of understanding, we should trust God and his goodness at all times.

* Bonus Activity *

(10 to 15 minutes)

If you have time, try this activity after "I'm Praying for You."

ASK:

- **With the shape the world is in today, how can God still be in control?**

SAY:

- **Situations around the world today give rise to many fears. The threat of terrorism, biological threats, wars and rumors of wars, militant extremists who seek to kill in the name of religion, despotic dictators who threaten their own people and the world, conflict in the Middle East, famine, civil wars, large-scale layoffs, stock market crashes, corporate and government scandals, and economic uncertainty scream at us from the daily headlines. It's enough to make a person wonder whether anyone can be safe or everything is spinning wildly out of control.**

  But Christians can be sure that God is still in control. None of this is too complicated or difficult for God to understand. He knows all the intricate details of every situation, and he is working out his will and plan for the world and for our individual lives.

ASK:

- **What problems have you seen in the news that stir controversy or seem beyond understanding or resolution?**

Divide the class into groups of two or three students. Have each group read Isaiah 46:9-11 and discuss how it relates to some of the problems the world is facing. Each group should select one of the problems mentioned and write a paraphrase of Isaiah 46:9-11, plugging in details about and assurances for the current situation.

SAY:

- **God can use even evil people and bad situations to accomplish his good purposes. No one—no dictator, no terrorist, no politician, no country—can thwart or slow down what God has planned from the beginning of time.**

Invite students to pray specifically for the situations you've discussed.

The Point ▶ Conclude with thanksgiving and praise to God that we can trust him to know what he's doing and to keep bringing good out of the chaos and evil in this world.

Person-Shaped Puzzle

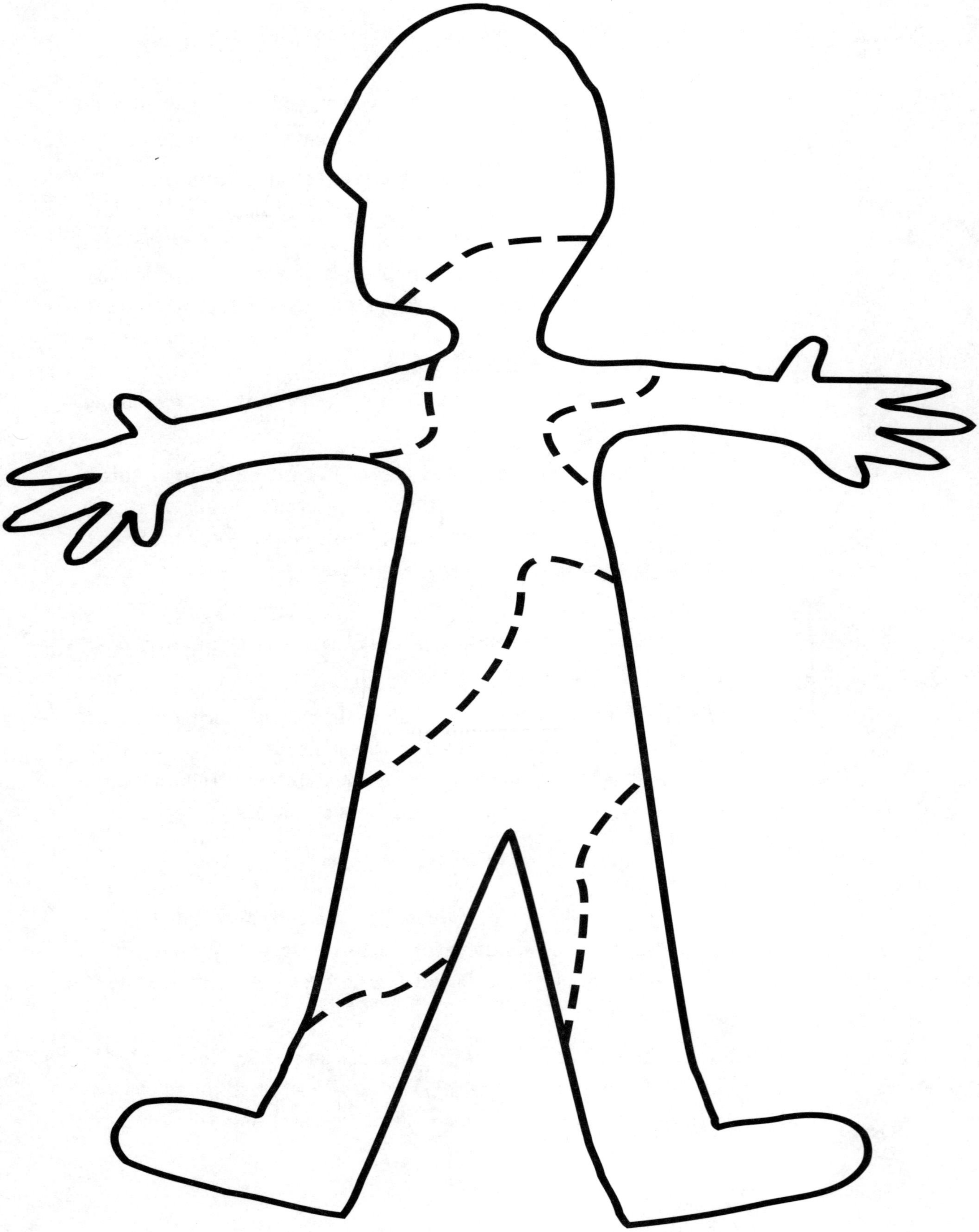

Jesus: The Ultimate Friend

Most teenagers spend as much time as possible with their friends. Often it seems everything in their lives revolves around friendship. They'll wear only what their friends would approve of. They spend hours talking over every detail of some turn of events at school or at a social gathering. They'll even base life decisions on their friends' opinions. Yet teenagers' circle of friends can change frequently because of some misunderstanding, hurt, or even betrayal. Because no one is perfect, teenagers' image of friendship can be less than perfect. They need to know that Jesus set the ultimate example of friendship and, most important, that he can be their best friend.

Through this study, teenagers will discover that Jesus is the best friend they'll ever have. They can learn to trust him. They'll also be challenged to follow his example. Teenagers can respond by dedicating themselves to follow Jesus' example, becoming a friend to others with Jesus' help.

The Point

▶ Jesus is the best friend you'll ever have.

Scripture Source

Mark 8:1-9; John 17:20-26; Ephesians 5:1-2; Philippians 2:5-11; Hebrews 13:5-6; 1 Peter 5:7

Jesus demonstrated characteristics that show he is our friend.

John 15:12-17

Jesus commands us to follow his example in loving and being a friend to others.

The Study at a Glance

Warm-Up (10-15 minutes)

Freeze Frame

What students will do: Present "freeze frames" that represent characteristics of true friends.

Needs:
- ❑ props
- ❑ costumes
- ❑ newsprint
- ❑ marker

Bible Connection (20-25 minutes)

The Lead Role

What students will do: Explore the Bible and create movie titles to discover ways that Jesus is a true friend.

Needs:
- ❑ Bibles
- ❑ scissors
- ❑ "Jesus, My Friend" handout (p. 25)

Bonus Activity (5-10 minutes)

What students will do: Create and perform promotional "movie clips" to advertise their movie titles about Jesus, the true friend.

Needs:
- ❑ paper
- ❑ pencils
- ❑ video camera (optional)

Life Application (15-20 minutes)

Coming Attractions

What students will do: Create movie posters about their life stories.

Needs:
- ❑ poster board or newsprint
- ❑ markers
- ❑ scissors
- ❑ rulers
- ❑ pencils
- ❑ tape
- ❑ glue
- ❑ construction paper
- ❑ magazines

Before the Study

Set out props in the middle of the room. Some examples include sports equipment, books, hats, clothing, shoes, jewelry, and wigs. Make one photocopy of the "Jesus, My Friend" handout (p. 25), and cut apart the sections of the handout.

Warm-Up

Freeze Frame

(10 to 15 minutes)

After all teenagers have arrived,

SAY:

- **I'd like you to think of one characteristic of a true friend. When you've thought of a characteristic, present a "freeze frame" with at least one other person representing that quality. In other words, strike a pose that makes you look as though you're doing something a true friend would do, then "freeze" yourself in that position. You may use the props I've provided or anything else in the room to complete your picture. After you've finish presenting your freeze frame, please make your props available for others to use.**

When teenagers have created their freeze frames, ask them each to explain their poses and the characteristics portrayed. List the characteristics on the board or newsprint as teenagers describe them. After everyone has presented his or her characteristic,

ASK:

- **Do our freeze frames present a complete picture of a friend?**
- **Who are some people (past or present) who exemplify true friendship?**
- **Can you think of any person who has all the characteristics represented here? If so, who?**
- **How do these characteristics compare with your friends?**
- **How do these characteristics compare with Jesus' character?**

SAY:

- **Because Jesus exemplifies all the characteristics of a true** friend, he is the best friend you'll ever have. Let's look at some specific characteristics of Jesus as a friend.

◀ **The Point**

Bible Connection

The Lead Role

(20 to 25 minutes)

Have teenagers form three groups. Give each group a section of the "Jesus, My Friend" handout (p. 25).

SAY:

- **For the next ten minutes, look up the Scripture references listed on your handout, and then discuss the questions and follow the directions on the handout.**

After ten minutes, ask volunteers from each group to share the group's movie title and explain how it connects with Jesus' characteristics. If time allows, have teenagers give short descriptions of the movies they've envisioned. Then have each group discuss the following questions.

ASK:

- **What did you discover about Jesus?**
- **How does Jesus compare with our idea of a friend today?**

Ask a volunteer to read aloud John 15:12-17. Then

ASK:

- **What does Jesus tell us about love in these verses? about friends?**
- **Why do you think Jesus calls us his friends?**
- **Do you think Jesus is your best friend? Why or why not?**
- **How would your life change if you always lived as if Jesus is the best friend you'll ever have?** ◀ **The Point**

*** Bonus Activity ***

(5 to 10 minutes)

If you have time, try this activity after "The Lead Role."

Have teams of students write and perform a brief promotional advertisement for their movie about Jesus, the friend. Challenge students to model their efforts after the movie trailers they see at the beginning of movies, videos, and DVDs. Students should consider these questions as they approach this fun project:

- **How will you make people interested in your movie?**
- **What exciting scenes about Jesus' friendship will you highlight?**
- **What approach will your movie promotion take to communicate the message of your movie?**
- **What appropriate props, visuals, theme songs, or effects can you add to make your promotion more appealing?**

If possible, provide a video camera (or a helper with a camera) to film your productions.

Life Application

Coming Attractions

(15 to 20 minutes)

Give each person a piece of poster board or newsprint. Set out markers, construction paper, pencils, rulers, tape, glue, magazines, and scissors.

SAY:

- **Draw a line three inches from the bottom of your paper. Below the line, use a marker to write in small letters, "Here's what the critics are saying!"**

After teenagers have drawn their lines,

SAY:

- **As a way of dedicating yourself to following Jesus' example, make a movie poster about the story of your life as if it were an upcoming movie. Include information about the characters and plot in your movie, the type of movie it will be, and the things people can learn from watching your movie. Be sure to think about your past as well as the kind of person you'd like to be in the future. Because <u>Jesus is the best friend you'll ever have</u>, include Jesus as one of the**

The Point ▶

characters in the movie, and show how he affects the movie's plot. Write only in the space above the line that you've drawn across the bottom of your poster. You have ten minutes to make your poster.

After ten minutes, have teenagers place their posters in a line on the floor. Give each person a marker.

SAY:

- **Walk down the line of posters, and use your marker to write on each person's poster one friendly characteristic you see in that person. Be sure to write your comments in the "Here's what the critics are saying!" section.**

When teenagers have finished writing their comments on the posters, close in prayer, praying that each person will learn to rely on Jesus for his or her ability to be a great friend to others.

Hang the movie posters on the walls of your classroom, or allow teenagers to take them home as reminders to follow Christ's example of friendship.

Jesus was popular in his contemporary culture, but he didn't fulfill the role people of his day expected him to. John 6:14-15 describes the reaction of the people to Jesus' feeding of the five thousand: "After people saw the miraculous sign that Jesus did, they began to say, 'Surely this is the Prophet who is to come into the world.' Jesus, knowing that they intended to come and make him king by force, withdrew again into the hills by himself."

Many of the people wanted and expected Jesus to be their friend and to come to their aid by conquering the Romans and taking charge of their society. Jesus knew that his mission on earth didn't include this kind of kingship. In fact, in Matthew 4:9, the devil tempted Jesus with this very option: "All this I will give you," he said, "if you will bow down and worship me." Jesus denied the temptation of kingship and kept to his task.

Jesus chose to be the friend and champion of the poor, the oppressed, the sick, and the dying. His mission of mercy culminated in his brutal death on a cross as he took the punishment for our sins. As God, Jesus humbled himself to the point of becoming human and dying in our place so we can be reconciled to God. In his life on earth, Jesus provided the ultimate example of friendship.

JESUS, MY FRIEND

GROUP 1

Read Philippians 2:5-11.

- According to this Scripture, what friendly qualities does Jesus have?
- Have these qualities affected your life? If so, how?

Read John 17:20-26.

- What do these verses say about the way Jesus sees you?
- What do these verses say about the way Jesus wants to relate to you?

Using the information from these two Bible passages, think of a title for a movie about Jesus. Make sure the title describes the characteristics of Jesus that you've discovered in these Bible passages.

GROUP 2

Read Ephesians 5:1-2.

- According to this Scripture, what friendly qualities does Jesus have?
- Have these qualities affected your life? If so, how?

Read 1 Peter 5:7.

- What do these verses say about the way Jesus sees you?
- What do these verses say about the way Jesus wants to relate to you?

Using the information from these two Bible passages, think of a title for a movie about Jesus. Make sure the title describes the characteristics of Jesus that you've discovered in these Bible passages.

GROUP 3

Read Mark 8:1-9.

- According to this Scripture, what friendly qualities does Jesus have?
- Have these qualities affected your life? If so, how?

Read Hebrews 13:5-6.

- What do these verses say about the way Jesus sees you?
- What do these verses say about the way Jesus wants to relate to you?

Using the information from these two Bible passages, think of a title for a movie about Jesus. Make sure the title describes the characteristics of Jesus that you've discovered in these Bible passages.

The Holy Spirit: River of Refreshing

The desert. A dry, barren wasteland with the sun beating down, withering everything in sight. What you wouldn't give for a drop of water in the desert!

Sometimes the world can feel like that, especially to today's young people. With society demanding so much from them yet giving them so few resources to meet those demands, teenagers can feel drained, thirsty for the tiniest drop of encouragement to make it through each day.

The good news is that a river runs through that teenage wasteland. If your students knew of it, they'd run to it and lap up all the water they wanted—and this river will never run dry.

What is this incredible river?

The Holy Spirit.

This study invites teenagers to find their way to the river—the Holy Spirit, our ever-present source of encouragement and help. Teenagers will explore the uses of water and compare water with the role of the Holy Spirit as encourager and helper. Through this comparison, teenagers will discover how the Holy Spirit can encourage them every day, especially through the tough times in their lives.

The Point

▶ The Holy Spirit encourages and helps you.

Scripture Source

John 7:37-39

Jesus describes the Holy Spirit as living water.

John 15:26; Acts 1:4-5, 8

Jesus tells the disciples he'll send the Holy Spirit to them after his death and resurrection.

Acts 9:31; Romans 8:9-13, 26-27

The Holy Spirit has many encouraging and helpful characteristics.

The Study at a Glance

Warm-Up (5-10 minutes)

Thirst Quencher

What students will do: Lick the salt off pretzels, then watch the leader drink a cup of water.

Needs:
- ❑ pretzels
- ❑ ice
- ❑ paper cups
- ❑ pitcher
- ❑ water
- ❑ markers

Bible Connection (25-35 minutes)

Living Water

What students will do: Explore the Scriptures about the encouraging and helping role of the Holy Spirit in Christians' lives.

Needs:
- ❑ Bibles
- ❑ pens
- ❑ water
- ❑ slips of paper
- ❑ cups
- ❑ "Thirst, Water, and the Holy Spirit" handouts (p. 35)

Bonus Activity (up to 5 minutes)

What students will do: Try to get cups of water off their backs.

Needs:
- ❑ paper cups
- ❑ water

Life Application (10- 15 minutes)

Encouraging Prayer

What students will do: Pray about ways they need the Holy Spirit's encouragement and help, then encourage one another as they give one another drinks of water.

Needs:
- ❑ cups
- ❑ water
- ❑ pens
- ❑ slips of paper from the "Living Water" activity

Before the Study

Make enough photocopies of the handout "Thirst, Water, and the Holy Spirit" (p. 35) so that each group of four can have one.

Warm-Up

Thirst Quencher

(5 to 10 minutes)

Begin the meeting by giving each student a pretzel.

FYI If your meeting room isn't close to a sink, fill several clean pitchers or buckets with water, and bring them to your room for easy access during this study.

SAY:

- **To begin today's study, let's have a contest to see who can lick the salt off a pretzel the fastest. When you've licked all the salt off your pretzel, raise your pretzel above your head to let me know. Ready? Get set. Go!**

When the first student raises a pretzel, inspect it to make sure he or she has licked off *all* the salt. If not, keep the contest going. When someone has won, sit in a circle with the group. Place a paper cup and a pitcher full of water and ice cubes in front of you. Then

ASK:

- **When have you been *really* thirsty?**

Allow teenagers to tell stories about times they were really thirsty, such as after running a race or while enduring a heat wave. Then tell the group a short story about a time you were thirsty and a simple glass of water (*not* a soft drink or a sports drink) quenched your thirst. At the end of your story, pour some ice water into the paper cup. Take a big gulp and

SAY:

- **Ahhhhhh.**

Then have teenagers form foursomes to discuss these questions:

- **What was your reaction to watching me take a drink of water after you'd licked the salt off your pretzel and told stories about being thirsty?**
- **How thirsty are you right now?**

- **How is being thirsty like needing help or encouragement? How is it different?**
- **When was one time you really needed someone to help or encourage you? What happened?**
- **How do you try to meet your needs for help and encouragement?**

While teenagers discuss the questions, pour water into paper cups, one cup per student. When groups have finished their discussions, hand each person a cup. As students drink their water,

SAY:

- **Sometimes life is like being thirsty. You need something to come in and refresh you. That's our focus today—finding something that can quench our spiritual thirst as water quenches our physical thirst. Through today's study, you'll discover how the Holy Spirit encourages and helps you.**

◀ **The Point**

FYI Because your students will drink a lot of water during this study, you may want to give them a bathroom break halfway through it.

Have students use markers to write their names on the outside of their cups. Tell them to keep track of their cups because they'll use them throughout the study.

Living Water

(25 to 35 minutes)

Bible Connection

Hand each student a slip of paper and a pen, and

SAY:

- **On the slip of paper I've just handed you, write one area of your life in which you're "thirsty" for encouragement or help. For example, you may feel discouraged because you're not doing as well in school as you'd like, or you may need comfort because a family member is really sick. Think of an area in which you need help *right now.***

FYI If you can think of a time the Holy Spirit comforted or encouraged you when you really needed it, tell your story to the class after teenagers have explored the Bible passages.

Give teenagers a moment to write their ideas, and then have them put their slips of paper into their pockets, socks, or shoes to refer to later.

Have teenagers return to their foursomes. Give each foursome a copy of the "Thirst, Water, and the Holy Spirit" handout (p. 35). Give students about twenty minutes to read the Bible passages, discuss the

FYI Non-Christian students may not know what believing in Jesus means. Be prepared to tell any students who approach you how they can have a relationship with Jesus Christ.

questions, and create a way to share what they've learned with the rest of the class.

Have groups act out their creative presentations of what they've learned from the study.

Then

SAY:

- **When you choose to believe in Jesus and develop a lifelong relationship with him, <u>the Holy Spirit encourages and helps you to grow</u>. Answer this question silently: Do you believe in Jesus? If you do, you can have all the encouragement and help you'll ever need. If you don't, perhaps you'd like to learn more about what believing in Jesus means. If so, you're welcome to talk to me after class.**

◀ The Point

FYI The Feast of Shelters (also called the Feast of Tabernacles or the Feast of Booths) was extremely important to the people of Jesus' day. All nations were exhorted to celebrate the festival each year and were warned that those who didn't would have no rainfall in the year ahead (see Zechariah 14:16-19). This exhortation and warning fell on the ears of people who knew the importance of water to their survival. The need for water was often the center of conflict at that time, and access to water was defended avidly.

Against this backdrop, Jesus described the Holy Spirit as "streams of living water" (John 7:38). Jesus chose to make this claim on the last, most important day of the Feast of Shelters–the day when everyone engaged in a water ritual to increase the chances of good rainfall throughout the coming year. By comparing the Holy Spirit to water in this context, Jesus helped people understand their need to satisfy their spiritual thirst. In John 7:37-39, Jesus claimed to have a better alternative to the water that people tried to gain through the ritual. By telling his listeners they could have "streams of living water" flowing from their hearts, Jesus was saying that the water he offers–the Holy Spirit–never runs dry.

* Bonus Activity *

(up to 5 minutes)

If you have time, try this Bonus Activity before "Encouraging Prayer."

SAY:

- **When you believe in Jesus, the Holy Spirit is always around to encourage and help you. Let's play a quick game that will illustrate this.**

Have students get on all fours on the floor. Fill each student's paper cup with water. Place the cup in the middle of the student's back.

SAY:

- **The object of the game is to get your cup of water off your back within thirty seconds, without spilling the water. Whoever does this first wins.**

When thirty seconds have elapsed or when someone has won,

SAY:

- **You may have been able to get your cup off your own back, but the easiest way to get the water off your back is to ask someone else to do it for you.**

Have students return to their foursomes to discuss these questions:

- **Were you able to get your cup of water off your back? If so, how?**
- **How were your attempts at getting the water off your back like the way you relate to the Holy Spirit when you need help or encouragement? How were they different?**
- **How is asking someone to take the water off your back like the way the Holy Spirit uses others to help or encourage you?**
- **Based on this game, will you change the way you seek help and encouragement when you need it? Explain.**

SAY:

- **Sometimes we really need help and encouragement. If we believe in Jesus Christ, we have the Holy Spirit inside us and have access to all the help and encouragement he can give. But often we don't even ask for it. If you belong to Jesus Christ, the Holy Spirit encourages and helps you whenever you need it, but you have to ask.**

◀ **The Point**

FYI

If you have more than ten teenagers, recruit one or two teenagers or adults to help you pour the water. When everyone else's water has been poured, have the recruited teenagers get down on all fours. Pour water into their cups, and place their cups on their backs.

FYI

If your students wear nice clothes to your youth meeting, lay plastic wrap on their backs before placing the cups of water on them.

Life Application

Encouraging Prayer

(10 to 15 minutes)

Again gather the group together.

SAY:

The Point ▶ ■ **When we need encouragement or help, we can pray and ask the Holy Spirit to encourage and help us. Let's practice this now.**

We're going to pray together in an unusual way. I'll start a prayer by praying the beginning of a sentence, and you will complete the sentence however you want. When you complete the sentence, you may say it aloud or to yourself.

PRAY:

■ **Dear God, we thank you because you are...**

After about fifteen seconds or when teenagers seem to have finished responding aloud,

PRAY:

The Point ▶ ■ **Holy Spirit, thank you for past times when you've encouraged and helped us—times such as...**

After about fifteen seconds or when teenagers seem to have finished responding aloud,

PRAY:

■ **Holy Spirit, we need your encouragement and help right now for situations such as...**

After about fifteen seconds or when teenagers seem to have finished responding aloud,

SAY:

■ **Amen.**

Have teenagers gather their cups, slips of paper from the "Living Water" activity, and pens. Then instruct teenagers to return to their foursomes, and have each foursome sit in a circle.

SAY:

The Point ▶ ■ **One way the Holy Spirit encourages and helps you is through one another. When you say encouraging words to one**

another, the Holy Spirit uses those words to quench your "thirst" for support and reassurance. Let's practice this now. In your group, think of something encouraging you can say to the person sitting on your left. For example, you can say, "I hope you do well on tomorrow's math test" or "You're a fun person to be with." Don't say your encouragement yet—just think about it.

As teenagers think, pour water into each person's cup. If you have more than ten students, recruit an adult leader to help you do this quickly.

When you've finished filling the cups,

SAY:

- **Pass your own cup to the person on your right. You should now be holding the cup of the person you're supposed to encourage. In your groups, each of you will take a turn to encourage the person on your left. As you say your encouraging words, hold that person's cup to his or her lips, and help that person drink. Make sure you don't spill!**

When teenagers have finished their encouragements,

SAY:

- **The water you helped one another drink is a symbol of the living water that the Holy Spirit can be for you. Look at the slip of paper you wrote on earlier. How can the Holy Spirit encourage and help you through that situation? On the back of the slip of paper, write one way you'll seek the Holy Spirit's encouragement and help this week. For example, you might choose to talk to someone about a problem and allow the Holy Spirit to encourage you through that person. Or you might choose to pray about the situation and actively look for an answer. When you've written your idea, share it with your group members.**

When groups have finished, have teenagers put their slips of paper in their cups (tell them to drink any lingering drops of water before doing so). Encourage teenagers to take their cups home as reminders that the Holy Spirit encourages and helps them.

◀ **The Point**

THIRST, WATER, AND THE HOLY SPIRIT

Read John 7:37-39.

- What does Jesus say about water in this story?
- Who is the water?
- How can you receive this water?

Read John 15:26 and Acts 1:4-5, 8.

- What gift is Jesus talking about?
- What does Jesus say this gift does?
- What can Jesus give you through the Holy Spirit?

Read Acts 9:31 and Romans 8:9-13, 26-27.

- What do these passages tell you about the Holy Spirit?
- Having read all the passages on this handout, what's one statement you can make about the Holy Spirit?
- Have you ever experienced a time you felt God, through the Holy Spirit, gave you encouragement and help? If so, what happened?
- Look at the slip of paper you wrote on earlier. What kind of encouragement do you wish the Holy Spirit would give you in that situation?

Now prepare to share what you've learned with the rest of the class.

Using water and/or your cups, think of a creative way you can communicate what you've learned about how the Holy Spirit can encourage and help you. For example, you can be a fountain of living water, pouring water from pitchers into your cups as you strike a pose and recite a verse. Or you can line up, each of you with your cup in your hand, and pass some water from one cup to the next as you list ways the Holy Spirit encourages and helps people.

BE CREATIVE!

God's Standard: Learning the Rules of Life

Today's society peddles the seductive idea that truth, right, and wrong are all subjective. Commercials, media, and even parents and teachers exhort teenagers to make up their own minds or to do what's right for them. The premise is that, depending on the situation and the people involved, something may be the truth for you but a lie for someone else. A belief or an action may be wrong for you but perfectly acceptable for another.

In this study, teenagers will learn that God is the only one with the authority and wisdom to make the rules about what's right and what's wrong. Truth is truth. Sin is sin. God is the one who has set the standard for acceptable human behavior. It may seem confusing when a thousand conflicting voices from the world distract us and seem to drown out God's truth, but God has given us three reliable avenues for learning his standards for every question we face in life: God's direct commands in his Word, Jesus' example, and the Holy Spirit's guidance.

The Point

▶God defines what is right.

Scripture Source

Nehemiah 9:6

Only God has the authority and wisdom to make the rules.

Psalm 119:9-16; John 14:26; 16:13; Hebrews 1:1-3; 1 Peter 2:21

God reveals the difference between right and wrong.

The Study at a Glance

Warm-Up (10-15 minutes)

Create a Game

What students will do: Make up a simple game complete with rules.

Needs:
- ❑ paper
- ❑ pencils
- ❑ markers

Optional Activity (10-15 minutes)

What students will do: Match the right rules to various games and recognize the importance of following the proper instructions.

Needs:
- ❑ several games
- ❑ multiple copies of the instructions with the name of the game blacked out

Bible Connection (25-30 minutes)

Rule Book, Play Review, and Coach

What students will do: Form three teams to study and teach three ways to know what's right by writing instructions, demonstrating, and teaching/guiding others to learn.

Needs:
- ❑ Bibles
- ❑ paper
- ❑ pens
- ❑ art supplies
- ❑ chalkboard
- ❑ chalk
- ❑ various teaching supplies
- ❑ "Rule Book, Play Review, and Coach" handout (p. 43)

Life Application (10-15 minutes)

Jeopardy!

What students will do: Find God's answers to relevant issues of right and wrong through commands and examples in the Bible.

Needs:
- ❑ "Jeopardy!" handout (p. 44)
- ❑ Bibles
- ❑ wrapped candies or self-adhesive notes

Bonus Activity (5-10 minutes)

What students will do: Develop a personal daily regimen of Bible study and prayer.

Needs:
- ❑ Bibles
- ❑ paper or cardstock
- ❑ pens

Before the Study →

Make a copy of the "Rule Book, Play Review, and Coach" handout (p. 43), and cut it into sections to use in the Bible Connection activity.

Make at least one copy of the "Jeopardy!" handout (p. 44). You'll want one copy for each group in the "Jeopardy!" activity. You may want to enlarge the handout so you can post it on the wall and everyone can see it.

Review the game instructions in the study so you're familiar with them before your youth meeting.

Warm-Up

Create a Game

(10 to 15 minutes)

Hand out paper, pencils, and markers; then divide the class into teams. Challenge each team to create an original game, complete with rules. Teams might make up simple action games similar to Tag, word games, sports, or simple board games. After five minutes, allow each team to explain briefly its game to the rest of the class. Focus on the rules stated. Ask for clarification when the rules seem unclear. Then

ASK:

- **What gives you the right to determine what's allowed and what's against the rules in your game?**
- **What if the pastor or the smartest scientist in the world told you the rules of the game were really something else?**
- **How is this like God deciding the "rules" for life?**

FYI: If you have time at the end of class, allow students to play the games they've created.

Discuss how in creating a game, we get to decide the rules. Then

SAY:

The Point ▶

- **If for no other reason than Creator's privilege, God would have that same authority to define what's right for all of creation.**

* Optional Activity

(10 to 15 minutes)

Instead of the "Create a Game" activity, try this variation. Bring in several board or card games that your students may know how to play. Make enough photocopies of the instructions for each group to have instructions for all the games. Black out (or cut out) the game's name from the instructions.

Have students form groups of two or four. Give each group one game and sets of instructions for all the games. Ask kids to try playing the game using various sets of instructions before choosing the correct instructions for that game.

ASK:

- **Why is it important to follow the right set of instructions?**
- **Why is it important to follow the right instructions for our lives?**
- **Who determines the rules for our lives?**
- **What would happen if we rejected God's rules in favor of whatever is popular in our society?**

Rule Book, Play Review, and Coach

Bible Connection

(25 to 30 minutes)

ave teenagers read Nehemiah 9:6.

ASK:

- **Besides being the Creator, what credentials does God have that give him authority to define what is right?**
- **When we know that God sets the rules, how can we discover what we need to know in our everyday lives to make choices that please God?**

SAY:

- **It's important to understand and acknowledge that who God is gives him the right to define what is right. God doesn't want it to be a secret. He has given us everything we need to tell right from wrong: God's direct instruction written in**

◀ **The Point**

his Word, the example of Jesus, and the guidance of the Holy Spirit.

Form three groups. Give each group a section of the "Rule Book, Play Review, and Coach" handout (p. 43). Instruct teenagers to study the Bible passage and follow the particular way they are to prepare to teach it to the rest of the class.

Give groups approximately five minutes to prepare and five minutes for each group to share its information with the class. Be sure to discuss some of the questions listed on the handout.

Life Application

Jeopardy!

(10 to 15 minutes)

Use the "Jeopardy!" handout (p. 44) to play a game with your group. You may want to enlarge the handout to play one game with the entire class (divided into two or three teams). If your group is large, have several games run simultaneously. If you post the game to a wall or board, cover each square with an appropriately sized piece of sticky paper to conceal the Scripture reference until the appropriate time.

Ask for a volunteer to keep score. Divide the rest of the class into two or three teams. Students will take turns selecting a square, removing the cover, and reading aloud the reference that's revealed. Everyone on both teams races to look up the verse as quickly as possible.

The points indicated on the game board are given to the team of the person who first finds and reads the verse aloud. The same number of points will be awarded to the team of the person who first comes up with a practical question about what's right that can be answered by that command or example from the life of Christ (for instance, for the reference Exodus 20:15, a suitable question might be, "Is it OK to use large portions of an article I found on the Internet for my essay?"). The same team can win the points twice, or two different teams can win points on each attempt.

Some squares have no reference, only the note, "The Holy Spirit guides us." When these squares are revealed, points are awarded for the team that can first come up with a situation in which its members might need the Holy Spirit's guidance to tell right from wrong. When you're done with the game, conclude the study with a time of prayer.

FYI If your class is small, consider placing the game board on a table and covering the references with candies instead of sticky notes. The student who selects the square wins the candy.

FYI This activity will help teenagers practice finding right answers through some of the means discussed in this study.

* Bonus Activity *

(5 to 10 minutes)

If you have time, conclude the Bible study with this Bonus Activity.

Have students read Isaiah 48:17-18.

ASK:

- **How can we know we're making the right choices?**
- **How can we learn to obey God's commandments?**

SAY:

- **If we want to have peace that comes from knowing we're making the right choices, we need to learn and obey God's commandments. To do this, we need to make daily prayer and Bible study a priority in our lives.**

Give students paper and pens. Allow them to work individually or in pairs to develop a realistic plan for personal daily devotions. Have them write the specifics of their plan. Ask the following questions to help teenagers develop a plan.

ASK:

- **When will you spend this time in prayer and Bible study?**
- **How long will you spend?**
- **Where will you do this?**
- **What study tools will you use?**
- **What Bible will you read?**

Encourage teenagers to keep a notebook or journal to write prayers and to record what they've learned. Then gather the entire class, and pray for one another. Pray that each student will have a desire to seek God and know his commands so he or she can know and do right.

RULE BOOK, PLAY REVIEW, AND COACH

God's Written Word

Passage: Psalm 119:9-16

<u>**Method for sharing this information:**</u> Rule book—written instruction—think through this passage, and explain to the rest of the class in writing the importance of God's Word in understanding God's definition of right and wrong and in applying that to our daily lives.

Be prepared to answer these questions:

- **What's the relationship between God's Word and a Christian's ability to do right?**
- **How can we become familiar with God's instructions?**
- **What roles do meditation and memorization have in learning God's laws?**
- **What should be a Christian's attitude and actions toward the Bible?**

GROUP 2

God's Word Revealed—Jesus, Our Example

Passages: Hebrews 1:1-3; 1 Peter 2:21

<u>**Method for sharing this information:**</u> Play review—showing visually—act out the passages, or explain them and give (or show) examples of how someone did right (or how we can know we're doing right) when we follow Christ's example.

Be prepared to answer these questions:

- **Who is our example?**
- **What's the relationship of Jesus to the Scriptures?**
- **Why can we see the Father through Jesus?**
- **What are some things Jesus' example shows us are right and good?**
- **What are some things his example shows us are wrong?**

The Counselor—The Holy Spirit Guides Us

Passages: John 14:26; 16:13

<u>**Method for sharing this information:**</u> Coach—teach, guide, help others read and understand the work of the Holy Spirit in helping us know right from wrong. Be a creative teacher.

Be prepared to answer these questions:

- **What are the names given for the Holy Spirit in these passages?**
- **What's the significance of these names in helping us determine right from wrong?**
- **From these verses, describe some of the roles of teacher that the Holy Spirit fulfills.**
- **How can the Holy Spirit help us discern God's standard of right and wrong?**
- **How does he help us interpret God's Word?**
- **How does he help us when we have to make a decision about something not specifically addressed in God's Word?**

Jeopardy!

$100	Exodus 20:15	Matthew 7:1-2	Matthew 5:43-44	Romans 13:1
$200	Luke 10:27	Exodus 22:21	Psalm 101:5	Matthew 5:21-22
$300	Romans 12:19-20	Matthew 5:27-28	Exodus 20:12	The Holy Spirit Guides Us
$400	The Holy Spirit Guides Us	Psalm 100:4	1 Timothy 6:17	Matthew 5:39
$500	1 Peter 4:9	1 John 2:9-11	2 Corinthians 6:14	Galatians 6:10

Changed 4 Life

To keep your students thinking about who God is, try this idea at the end of the last study.

Announce the date, approximately a month in the future, of a fine arts festival. Challenge students to use any fine arts medium to demonstrate what they've learned during the course of this study about who God is.

Categories to consider include the following:

- **Writing (essay, poetry, story, song)**
- **Drawing**
- **Painting**
- **Photography**
- **Sculpting**
- **Crafting**
- **Human video**
- **Movie making**
- **Singing**
- **Creative movement**
- **Scrapbook making**
- **Baking**

Challenge students to use what they've learned about God to enter at least one category, but hopefully several. Entries may focus on one member of the Trinity (God the Father, Jesus, or the Holy Spirit) or on all three.

Invite parents, friends, and church members to watch performances and view entries. You may wish to serve refreshments and reward outstanding entries, or give treats to all who entered.

Be sure to take some time to review what the entries show about who God is.

Student Plan-It Devotional Organizer

New Expanded Size!
More, Bigger Pages!
New Durable Cover!

What is it? A calendar. An encouraging devotional. A journal. A place to store contact information (phone numbers, emails and more). Includes wacky holidays, interesting facts, and practical life tips.

Student Plan-It Devotional Organizer
This easy-to-use planner is crammed full of cool stuff students need!

And, it's convenient . . .

- It's a calendar.
- It's an inspiring and encouraging devotional.
- It's a journal (expanded size allows more space than ever!)
- It's where you store contact information (phone numbers, e-mails and more).
- It includes practical life tips and helps for studying, handling stress and relationships.
- It includes wacky holidays to celebrate as well as interesting, little-known facts.

Help Students Grow Deeper in Faith—and More Organized at the Same Time!

It's the perfect gift for back-to-school, birthdays, graduation, or anytime you want to help your students feel special—and grow closer to God.

ISBN 0-7644-2455-6 $12.99

Visit your local Christian bookstore,
or contact Group Publishing, Inc., at 800-447-1070.
www.grouppublishing.com